D0735851

also by rachel zucker

the pedestrians

the pedestrians

rachel zucker

WAVE BOOKS

SEATTLE/NEW YORK

Published by Wave Books

www.wavepoetry.com

Wave Books titles are distributed to the trade by

Consortium Book Sales and Distribution

Phone: 800-283-3572 / SAN 631-760x

Library of Congress Cataloging-in-Publication Data

Zucker, Rachel.

[Poems. Selections]

The pedestrians / Rachel Zucker.

pages cm

ISBN 978-1-933517-90-2 (hardback)

ISBN 978-1-933517-89-6 (trade paperback)

I. Title.

PS3626.U26P44 2014

813'.6—dc23

2013034614

Designed and composed by Quemadura

Printed in the United States of America

9 8 7 6 5 4 3 2 1

First Edition

Wave Books 044

fables

the pedestrians

fables

For Joshua, my animal

the other city

One summer they decided to take their children to a faraway city that was completely unlike the city in which they lived.

Everything was very expensive and no one smiled unless it was absolutely necessary. The buildings were grandiloquent and everywhere remnants of the defunct aristocracy glimmered behind the scrim of *joie de vivre*. The denizens of this city loved food and clothing even more than the denizens of their own city loved food and clothing, and this seemed a superior and enlightened way of living.

"Yes," she thought, through a haze of jet lag, "there should be no limits placed on the value of a very fine cheese."

But soon the gluttonous monotony of ordering the perfect food at the most *au courant* restaurant very late at night among slim metropolitans who smoked while casually wearing unnecessary scarves began to seem obsessively consumptionistic, and she began to wish that the devoted patrons of *la meilleure boulangerie* would go home and eat less-than-sub-lime bread or imperfectly cooked rice, go to sleep early, and have regular dreams.

Day after day she dragged the children from sight to sight and night after night lay in bed with the husband and thought about how, despite the many carousels and the *verveine* tea and the peaches that tasted like peaches (and would forever ruin the tasteless peaches available in the city that was her city), this city was more like her city than any other place on earth. She knew then that the patriotism her children were developing as a result of this voyage, a patriotism born of their hatred for long tours of national monuments and their hatred for the unexpectedly barbarous native children and for the native adults who hated children, especially the children of foreigners—this patriotism was false. It was false and *artificiel* not because their feelings were unfounded but because the whole notion of dissimilitude was illusory.

She lay next to the snoring husband in the sublet bed and realized that though the bedroom smelled like smoke and the wooden floors of the bathroom smelled like her three sons' urine (and why anyone would use wood rather than tile or stone or linoleum or something easily washable for a bathroom floor was beyond her)—she realized that this city, so unlike her city, was exactly like her city and that everyone in her city was exactly like everyone in this city and that they were all animals and that animals can only be animals.

Many days passed. Many nights. The same number of days and nights. They slept in the smoke-drenched bed or rather the husband snored and sputtered and she lay awake and unseeing under her chilled eye mask. They tried keeping the long windows closed. It was quieter then but stuffy. Nothing they did seemed to quell the smell of cigarettes that neither of them smoked.

She had a small copper wire inside her. This made conception highly unlikely. She longed for the possibility of reproduction even though she didn't want another child. Without the chance of another child, sex lost some of its appeal, purposefulness, danger, pleasure, mystery, productiveness. This was difficult to explain to the husband because he didn't feel that way and wasn't made that way.

"We're animals," he says, happily, after sex.

"No," she thinks. Not anymore.

There is a shape stuck on the window screen.

"You have to see this," the husband says.

"Spiders," she says when she sees it. It is two stick-like spiders overlapping on the outside of the screen.

"Oh," he says.

She had something and wanted to put it down. But it was nighttime and, as always, the husband lay next to her, sleeping. She didn't want to wake him. She didn't want to further rouse herself and invite a long night of insomnia. Still, she was afraid to lose the small new something. She hoped she could leave it, like a penny on a train track, and in the morning return to find what new shape the wave of sleep had left. But, would she remember?

ocean

She sat on the deck, face in the shade, legs in the sun, reading books by people in the faraway city. She'd cry a little or watch a small mammal run across the road.

Once she was on the phone with a poet who lived on the other coast, and she described the creature she thought was a beaver, woodchuck, or hedgehog. The poet on the other coast assured her, with great confidence, that it was a woodchuck. He explained that woodchucks' legs are designed for hills and that's why when running on flat ground the animal looked as if he were hopping on his back legs.

"Totally," she told the poet even though she didn't even know the names of the animals or birds or trees or flowers and had trouble sitting still and spent most of her time wondering why she was reading sad memoirs.

Every day she watched the UPS truck come toward her up the road, make a three-point turn into the driveway before hers, and pull away.

It rains and rains. It rains. He sits there reading. She sits in the other part of the room, reading. They cannot see one another but can hear each other if they shout. After a while they get up and close all the windows. He closes the windows upstairs and she closes the windows downstairs. They sit down again and everything is quiet except for the sound of rain and occasional thunder.

"Somebody died," he says.

"Who?" she says.

"Some girl," he says. "I didn't really know her. I can't even picture her."

"That's terrible," she says.

It rained.

Later, it rained.

"Actually, I totally know who this is!" he says.

"Who?" she says.

"This *girl*! I'm shocked!"

"That's terrible," she says.

They were sitting on the deck having that same difficult conversation they had every few months no matter where they were or what else was happening.

The husband said he felt he'd wasted many previous summers and how did that make her feel?

He said he had nothing to show for himself and what did she think of that?

She thought of fox trying to reach a bunch of delicious-looking grapes on the high vine. The trunk was too straight, the bark too smooth, the first branch too high.

Everything about the tree was unhelpful, wrote one of Aesop's translators.

"I'm not angry," she says.

"That's the first nice thing you've said all day," she says.

"I *am* listening," he says.

"When you ask me what's wrong, *that's* what's wrong," he says.

"I don't care if you write a children's book," he says.

"Don't laugh at me," she says.

"I *was* trying to help you," he says.

"Stop talking," say the children.

Sometimes her heart would beat a bit faster or irregularly as if her body was fighting back, clinging to wakefulness. Mostly, though, she enjoyed the feeling of the sleeping pill taking hold, pulling her toward quietude. It was foreplay with a predictable outcome. So unusual: that kind of kept promise.

Once there was a jackdaw black as soot with a bright eye, a voice like a broken bell, and some nasty habits she couldn't help. More and more she looked like her mother. Same expressions, similar fears and aspirations. This summer everyone seemed able to hurt her feelings even with small offenses. The husband hated it when she cried. Her scrunched wet face made him feel helpless and feeling helpless made him angry and his anger made him mean. She would then accuse *him* of being unhappy and decide that she was in this—meaning life—all alone and couldn't rely on him for anything and for days would go about dry-eyed with a hard aloofness, her chin slightly raised, arms crossed over her chest. But these were the feathers of other birds and neither she nor the husband had any patience for finery, which they both considered pretentious and inauthentic. So they'd kerfuffle and say hurtful things and all her carefully assembled armature would fall away. Then she would appear again as the ordinary jackdaw he loved.

Whenever she sat down to say something she heard someone moving around in the other room. True, it was raining, but it wasn't the sound of rain. It was the sound of someone moving around in the kitchen or in the bathroom next to the kitchen even though no one was there.

"Feel how hard I am," the husband said, putting aside the pornographic novel.

"Huh?" she said, not moving or looking up at him from the novel she was reading, a novel about a man building a machine to bring his beloved brother back from the dead.

They had not known each other when they were teenagers but when the radio with the human genome played Phil Collins it was 1985 bar mitzvah season all over again.

"This is a slow-dance song," the husband said.

She stopped wiping down the counters and put out her hand. They slow-danced in the middle of the kitchen, both thinking of how their couple's therapist had cajoled them for so many years to dance together and they always refused and it became a kind of joke between them and the therapist.

But, in the kitchen, they did dance together: soberly, slowly. She felt the husband's soft penis through his shorts, against her thigh. The husband put his hand on her ass. She closed her eyes and tried not to think about how in 1985 bar mitzvah season she'd been awkward and shy and was hardly ever asked to dance. She tried not to think about how on the rare occasions when she was asked, she mostly refused. She tried not to think about how on the rare occasions she accepted an invitation, she was not able to overcome the feeling that everything about her body was effortful and ungraceful. She'd come to hate dancing and being asked and not being asked and had never quite gotten over this and had married a man who didn't like to dance—a man who, as Phil Collins crooned "I've been waiting for this moment for all my life ...," laughed nervously and said too loudly in her ear, "I can't do this—." "Look here," she thought, "I sing like a rusty gate."

They sat on the deck at the end of a dead-end street a few blocks from the ocean. After a time they could see the mail truck heading toward them down the small road. She had been meaning to mention her feelings about the mail truck to the husband but kept forgetting to.

The husband was talking about *Hamlet* and then Philip Roth and then about how he'd made several grave misjudgments in his life and with his time.

"It seems so sad," she said. "When it turns around—" but stopped, knowing from his face that she'd made a mistake.

"What are *you* waiting for?" he snarled.

He had a snake tongue then. She saw it slip back into his mouth and felt the sting of his fangs, the poison of his disappointment. It was always there like the creek behind the house—sometimes inaudible, sometimes burbling through the quiet nights—always, no matter how dry the season: a carved-out trench where nothing good could grow.

She had been waiting all summer. When it arrived, it was difficult to find her quiet mind. During the day it was hard to hear what the children were asking for. At night she thought longingly of sleeping pills.

One evening the husband yelled, "Ew! You smell like a rotten egg!"

The husband yelled, "Disgusting! Disgusting! Disgusting!" as he rolled around with their little boy, tickling him and smelling the little boy's feet. The little boy laughed and shrieked and laughed so hard he struggled to catch his breath.

"Stop!" begged the boy, who wanted it to go on forever.

She wiped down the counters in the kitchen, surprised to feel a nut of envy hardening in her belly. She wanted to be touched that way. No, not *that* way.

They were waiting. The hurricane was gathering strength and slowly heading toward them—directly through their own great city and then on toward the place they were currently living. The slowness of the storm was a problem. It could stay in one place long enough to cause sustaining damage.

At first she heard they should close and lock and tape up all the windows. She wondered about this, about whether it might be better to allow a tiny opening that might act as a kind of pressure-relief valve. The husband said they should fill the rented minivan with gas but otherwise shouldn't worry. She wondered. Then the radio said they should *not* tape the windows, that taping the windows was more dangerous than not taping the windows. She waited for the experts to change their minds about closing and locking the windows but either they didn't change their minds or else the kids were fighting and she missed the announcement.

The radio said an eleven-year-old boy was killed when a tree fell through his bedroom window. The husband said every-

one should sleep in his own bed and anyway the storm wasn't
coming until Sunday.

Of course she worried. She didn't know how to be an oak tree
or a reed. The radio said: "The wind isn't the problem, the wa-
ter is."

It was hard to say goodbye to the ocean. It was not the same ocean as it had been the day before. Today the waves crashed against her, pushing her back toward shore. At the same time the tide was going out and tried to pull her with it. It was hard work just standing her ground. She wanted to say, "I love you." She wanted to say, "Thank you." But to whom? To which part? The part of the ocean that was trying to push her away or the part that wanted to swallow her?

apartment

She wanted to believe that she could write the way some women sat knitting. She wanted to make something out of peacefulness but worried that peacefulness was antithetical to makefulness.

"Play," her friend said over the phone.

She asked the computer for a tarot reading and the computer told her staves and pentacles: rest, happiness, joy, stability.

"Idle hands," she thought, but there was no one there to argue with.

She laid her hands palms-up in her lap and waited.

All night long her breath came and went too quickly. She was filled with hatred for the husband she loved so dearly. Her breath caught now and then as if she'd been running a long way but there she was, lying in bed. It was too strong a word—*hatred*—and inaccurate. But nothing in her life had prepared her for how this felt and no word in her language described it.

One day she tied a $10 bill around the thin, braided trunk of a small money tree she'd bought at the farmer's market. The tree was scrawny and asymmetrical and was the only money tree the seller had. She'd made a joke about the poor economy and scarcity of money trees, but the plant man said, "Want it?" without smiling.

Sometimes when a breeze rustled the tear-shaped leaves they sounded like pages turning. Once she sat in a chair near the little plant, holding a book, waiting for the breeze. She wanted to turn the pages of her book and compare the sounds, but it was a still day and she lost patience with the experiment.

A colored spike of light reached up into the darker-than-day city night. Because it was closer to them than the building for which their city was most famous, this new building looked bigger than the building that was the only building left standing that really stood for her famous city. Whereas the colors of the famous building changed nightly or weekly for various state or local holidays or in memoriam for famous people or in honor of diseases, this new brightly colored spike changed every few minutes. She watched it—blue, green, orange, red— trying to discern a pattern.

"Where did that new building come from?" she asked the husband when he came into the bedroom.

"What building?" he joked, looking at the gaudy spike.

"Open?" he asked.

"No," she said, and he pulled down the shades.

When her mother invited her to go see the renowned Buddhist monk she said no. She didn't want to get a babysitter and she didn't want to go see a Buddhist monk.

She did not change her mind when her mother said, "It's important," or when her mother said, "He has an amazing presence," or when her mother said, "It would mean a lot to me."

"No," she said. "I'm sorry."

When she got to the conference center there were two long lines of people. One line of people all looked like her mother even though they were men and women, young and old, of all races. The other line was mostly young people dressed in leather with bleached hair. That line was for a pole-dancing competition. The people who looked like her mother were there for the Buddhist monk. As the lines funneled into adjacent doors, the two groups eyed each other hungrily.

Inside, nuns and monks were seated cross-legged on the stage. The chanting went on a long time and made her tired.

When the chanting was over, the Buddhist monk spoke about staying in the present, about anger, about breath. She wanted to know how she had come to be here after saying no and no and no. She wanted to know how long the monk would go on speaking. If there was a present—and she was not sure that there was—it was made of anger.

She practiced the guitar every day and took lessons once a week with her son's teacher. The tips of the fingers of her left hand hurt all the time. On the subway she liked to press them gently and feel the pain swell up. The pain made her feel young and ambitious. Then she stopped.

One night while making fish tacos she burned the tip of her index finger flipping tortillas without a spatula. It hurt for days but gave her no pleasure.

One day she found herself in a room in a building not far from the apartment where she and the husband and their children lived and had lived for all of their children's lives.

There were three desks, two windows, a small patio, kitchen and bathroom and a few books. Sometimes she sat and listened to the hum of the refrigerator. Other times she got up and closed the kitchen's pocket door and listened to the muffled hum of the refrigerator.

Sometimes a husband and a wife sat at the other two desks, with their backs to her. It was another husband and wife with their own quirks and disappointments. Usually that husband listened to headphones as he typed but that wife did not. Every once in a while that wife would say something to that husband and that husband would take off his headphones and she would repeat what she had just said.

Sometimes she sat there thinking about what it meant to be alive in one physical location instead of another, at one moment of time instead of another, to be one kind of animal rather than another. Other times she would pull the pocket door over that kind of thinking and sit and listen to the muffled sound of that kind of thinking while she made a clicking noise on her keyboard.

She is reading a book about a woman and her husband and their three children who are running away from an uprising in their city. It is difficult to figure out whom the novel is about and what if any of it is true, but the voice gets into her head.

At night, after reading, her mind says:

"She is lying in bed alone, the snoring husband banished to the red couch in the family room where he might be using pornography—"

Or,

"She goes to sleep on the seat taken from the broken-down bakkie as the husband listens to the radio for news of the uprising—"

It is not that she is hearing voices but that her thoughts have become inflected and unfamiliar. As sleep makes its approach she slips in and out of the other woman's story—surely her own three children are not lying on the damp dirt floor of a mud hut in a rural village. This is now the only way she leaves her city.

Sometimes, at night, when she turns away from him, it is obvious what she wants. The backside of her body is itself an invitation. Other times she turns away to give her left shoulder a rest or because that part of the pillow is too hot.

mountains

One day she got in a car and drove. It was not until she was on the highway that she was sure she would have the courage to do it. While she was driving she thought, "I am going," and that was all she knew.

She passed a deer on the side of the highway, its legs stiff and at odd angles. Later she passed a deer grazing on the median. She thought, "That is a live deer," and thought if she had not seen the dead deer first she would have just thought, "Deer."

She thought, "I am going." She thought, "I am on my way." She had two bags of hastily chosen books in the trunk of the car.

Later a hawk carrying a mouse in its talons flew across the frame of her windshield. "Wildlife," she thought, wondering what it felt like to be a half-dead mouse flying through the air.

Mountains appeared before her. They had always been there, of course, but were unseeable from her usual vantage point in her apartment in her city. Well, here they were. They seemed to be blocking her way and grew bigger as she drove toward them.

"I'm going," she thought. The mountains looked as real as a photograph.

In the town she bought two avocados, red grapes, two kinds of soup, kale cakes, two teriyaki chicken thighs, a chocolate bar with almonds and sea salt, a whole kabocha squash, wasabi rice chips, peanut butter, and a loaf of bread. At a different store she bought another soup. Soup seemed important. She bought a small salt grinder filled with pink salt. She bought a d'Anjou pear. If anyone asked her if she wanted bread with that she said yes. She said she did not need any plastic spoons. She got back in the car that was not her car and drove to the house that was not her house and put the three soups in a line on the counter and put the chicken, avocados, peanut butter, kale cakes, and other perishables into the refrigerator. The salt she had bought was, according to its brown eco-label, from the Himalayas and the purest salt on earth. It was "primordial" and was "created 250 million years ago during a time of pristine environmental integrity" and was "free of impurities unlike refined table salt or salt from today's oceans."

She sat and looked out at the sloping lawn and the mountains with their leafless deciduous trees and needled conifers and realized that this took even more courage than she'd expected. She turned the top of the salt grinder a few times and shook the contents onto her palm. The uneven crystals glittered like drugs or a geode's innards. When she licked her palm she felt her tongue come alive to the sharp, sweet tingle, and under that, the familiar taste of her own skin.

The online tarot reading says she already has everything she needs.

So, she gets quiet. When the phone rings she doesn't answer it. She makes a list of the things she thinks she lacks but might require: the ability to draw, a career as a singer . . .

The list or the making of the list is unendurable.

These are not her mountains.

Anyway she doesn't want mountains, doesn't understand mountains, including these mountains. Somewhere the ocean lies dark and lapping. It is winter everywhere.

When the fire goes out she wonders whether it is the light or warmth or noise she misses most. "This is who I am," she thinks, "in the end." But it is not the end.

The night is so dark and the surrounding woods so quiet there is nothing to interfere with the house's low mechanical drone. One person in one-half of one bed in one room of a many-roomed house, she thinks of the molecules of warm air agitated to keep her comfortable—some seeping out of door-jambs and window frames—moving in and around the cooler, untreated air of the vast interior of the medium-sized house.

When she wakes up the sky is white and overcast. The mountains are visible but nothing says "Go out into it" about the day, and the house has so many kinds of quiet.

What does it matter, she thinks, if she goes out? What does it matter if it is day or night?

It rained a little as if to confirm her suspicions. Sometimes mist settled into the cleft of the mountains so that when she lay on the floor and looked out the window it was as if she were seeing the world from an airplane. As the light began to fade she put on her jacket and shoes and tramped to the woodpile. From there she could see the pond, which had a strange, milky center. If she'd gone closer she might have determined whether it was ice or mist, but the wood was already heavy in her arms and she turned her back on the pond and went toward the house.

After that the sun, which she hadn't seen all day, set rapidly, and the white sky turned gray then ultramarine, and the trees and the mountains and houses turned black against the sky. Everything turned black except the clouds.

The fire caused the logs to steam and smoke. It caused the bark on the top log to curl like the skin of a fish fillet placed in a hot pan. The edges of the bark whitened and then glowed amber. There was something reptilian about the log. When the wood was reduced to ashes she put a fresh log on the half-burned ones. She would not let the fire die until all the timber she'd brought in was burned to ash. Why?

She needed neither heat nor light. She knew then how much she wanted something, anything, to happen.

the lark and her young ones

He could see it in the way she pressed her lips together. He could hear it in her sighing. He suspected she was often counting silently to herself. He couldn't imagine what she was not saying while she was counting (if she was counting) or what might happen if she stopped counting and sighing and pressing her lips together.

Sometimes she said she wanted to go to the hospital and be taken care of. Or else she wanted to be sequestered as a juror in a motel for several months. Also, when she'd gone for three days to stay in the house that was not her house where she could see the mountains she was none too fond of because what she really liked to look at was the ocean, she said she had not, at the end of the three days, wanted to come home.

Someone kept taking pens off her bedside table. Perhaps she was moving the pens and then forgetting she had moved them. It could have been the husband or one of the children but they didn't like the kind of pens she liked, and she never saw anyone in the narrow space between her side of the bed and the wall. Still, on the rare mornings she woke with lingering dreams she could not find the pens she was sure she'd left on the small table and though she cradled the dream in the half-dark like a baby bird to her desk in the other room it would fly off before she was able to record it. She was left with only an image of herself with very long hair or the feeling of pulling twine against a sheep's woolly muzzle.

She sits on the patio, the big red book resting on her legs, which are stretched out in front of her and propped up on a wooden stool. The red book contains a dead man's drawings, dreams, rants, and visions and causes her lingering unease. Whether the unease is caused by familiarity or strangeness she cannot discern.

"Even the eternal stars are commonplace," wrote the man.

"Be patient with the crippledness of the world and do not overvalue its consummate beauty," he wrote.

"One should not turn people into sheep, but sheep into people."

She copies his phrases into her notebook and watches a black-bodied insect scuttle over the patio's wooden planks. She looks at her feet, which look too big to be hers. She watches the spinning whirlybirds on the water tower across the way.

Her dreams had a recurring feeling, a theme almost, of surprise.

Oh! I didn't know I was pregnant and here I am nine months along!

All these years I've been married to that tall neighbor I always disliked!

Not exactly surprise—her language didn't have the word for the opposite of *déjà vu*.

Je ne suis jamais vu, she thought. *Je ne suis jamais.*

She wondered if certain feelings had objective as well as personal meaning the way, in a woman's dream, a man is often the animus and a woman is usually a shadow. The way the horse is libido and the snake is knowledge. The way she feels, every time, each time she sees her children.

First her elbow hurt. Then her wrist. Then fingers. Her shoulder and then her elbow again. She read a book that said each age had its maladies and pain was the body's way of stopping the mind from paying attention to something. She went running and thought, "My body is healthy and strong," all through the arm-aching run. Later, in the shower, she thought, "I do not want to think about ___," and the pain went away.

Then it came back.

So she lay down on a hard pallet, which slid into a metal tube. The tube shook and rattled and clanged. She did not open her eyes. "Hold perfectly still," the technician scolded through the ear-wear.

The technician gave her a button to press if she needed to press it and told her not to press it. She did not open her eyes. She felt the smooth surface of the button but did not press it.

"I do not want to think about ___," she thought, and inside the vibrating, clanging tube her pain became excruciating. She did not press the button. She wondered what the technician would see in the places no one could touch her.

From the air her city is veined with rivers and waterways, the promise of the ocean everywhere. The light glances off the afternoon skyscrapers, a peachy scrim between horizon and clouds smudged at their edge of meeting.

Bridges curve like snakes along the skin of land and water. Below her the grounded planes perch in strange formations, wings pert and ready. Buses and trucks bound the raceways like chummy canines. Police cars scuttle past streetlamps whose cyclopean, compound eyes shine demurely from long, bent necks.

She traverses the bowels of a chambered building and climbs into a four-wheeled machine. Out along the gray-backed highway, she rides. Through the millipede tollbooth and toward the municipality.

The early spring trees are hardened coral exposed by a tide that long ago went out and never returned. When she looks at them, the blocky elementary schools freeze like frightened lizards. All the eyes of all the creatures turn on as the sun goes down behind the rocks and hard-roofed play structures of the park's reptilian back.

She rides past the green fish-mouths of subway stairwells, along the twisted arteries of the megalopolis.

After several years of practice she was able to be alone, almost anywhere, for two to three minutes, but that was the limit of that. Otherwise, everyone was always asking, in his own way, when it was time to be afraid.

It's never safe to stay, she wanted to say. *There is no such thing as leaving.* But she swallowed her words as the season came once again into fullness. The wheat grew so ripe that when the wind shook the stalks, a hail of grains rustled down upon them.

There was no going away. Wherever she went they were with her.

the pedestrians

For my father and for my mother
who made me a pedestrian

Where then are the private turns of event
Destined to boom later like golden chimes
Released over a city from a highest tower?
The quirky things that happen to me, and I tell you,
And you instantly know what I mean?

—john ashbery

today my son told me

once long ago everything
grew everywhere all over
the planet people ate things
& dropped
what later became known as
SEEDS
they started to notice
things grew in certain places
where they'd dropped
what later became known as
SEEDS
that's called cultivation
my son explained
& used the word
CROPS
he said *crops changed everything*
hominids could stay in one place
and fence animals
this was the birth of culture

people didn't need to
gather & hunt all day
so they developed language
& the ability
to kill everything

real poem

Woke up. First big snow making
a new light—said that
before. Can't write—children—
said that. Get up:
food, oxygen. Seen snow before.

egg dream

I have four or maybe five eggs on the counter. I am preparing
to make something. What if they roll off?

mindful

jammed my airspace w/ a podcast &
to-do list filled up inside I run & running
then a snowstorm so no school I cried & said
*Mayor Bloomberg should be scalded with hot
cocoa* when someone said *Yay for snow!* I'm
cutting it too close Erin if a blizzard makes me
cry I used to long for snow for that quiet filling
everything up *What are you talking about?* asks Erin
Seriously what are you talking about? crammed
in the toddler bed I say *If you want me to stay
you need to lie still* the toddler tries why? must he?
is this what I was waiting for this one nap moment
of silence? if that's what I wanted I should have made
other don't you think choices? *What do you mean
by 'dark'?* asks Erin *What do you mean by 'in-
tolerable'?* I give one son a quarter for 2-or-fewer
complaints a day & none for more the pediatrician
confirms they each have 2 testicles then shoots
the smallest boy in the arm that was the easiest part
of my day is it NY? the lack of human contact?

oh *please* have no time for *that* got to go to sleep
by 10pm or am up all night something about
circadian rhythms then it's toddler-early-waking
Still night! we tell him *Not time!* timing time *Not time
to wake up!* we tell him *Go back* he won't we're up
it's dark *What are you saying?* texts Erin *Can't talk*
I text back but want to ask why is this life so run-
run-run long underground train then crosstown bus
that is *my* son w/ his 50 small feet kicking screaming
Too slow bus! Meredith says *The breath is the only thing
          in your life*

                    that takes care of itself does it? I know
time isn't 'a *thing* one has' I meant to ask isn't there
a way Erin to get more not time but joy? she's maybe
running or at the grocery or school can you
anyone hear me? my signal pen airway failed GPS
time left or *time left* I've forgotten to *oh!* left my *urgh!*
meat in the freezer or oven on so what? don't
make dinner? ha ha who will? the military?

real poem (infanticide)

In poems, some poets do bad things
to babies. This is called imagination.
I have babies and no imagination.

day care dream

Josh is a graduate student again. There's a place on campus that offers on-site childcare. There is also a place, next door to the childcare center, where I can leave fillets of fish in various tanks of marinade and pick them up later. I drop Judah off quickly but struggle at the fishmonger. I keep putting my fillets in the wrong kind of marinade. The woman in charge is short-tempered and offended by my ignorance of fish species. My slowness causes a line to form behind me. I'm deeply ashamed.

i'd like a little flashlight

& I'd like to get naked & into bed & be
HOT radiating heat from the inside these
blankets do nothing to keep out the out keep
my vitals in some drafty body I've got in & out
in all directions I'd like to get naked into bed but
HOT on this early winter afternoon already
dusky grim & not think of all the ways
I've gone about the world & shown myself
a fool shame poking holes in my thinned carapace
practically lacy woefully feminine I'd like to get
naked into bed & feel if not hot then weightless I
once was there was a sensory-deprivation tank
Madison WI circa 1992 I paid money for that
perfectly body-temperatured silent pitch-dark tank
to do what? play dead & not die? that was before
e-mail before children before I knew anything
just the deaths of a few loved ones which were
poisoned nuts of swallowed grief but nothing of life
or life giving which cuts open the self bursting busted
unsolvable I'd like to get naked into the bed of my life

but hot ʜᴏᴛ my little flicker-self trumped up somehow
blind & deaf to all the dampening misery of my friends' woes
I'd like a little flashlight to write poems w/ this lousy day
not this poem I'm writing under the mostly flat
blaze of bulb but a poem written w/ the light itself
a tiny fleeting love poem to life a poem that says
Look here a bright spot of life oh look another!

plant dream

My window plant is growing well. It's out on a fire escape I never knew I had. I say to Josh, "If I just forget about it and leave it alone, it does really well." I turn the plant so the thriving part faces inside. When I do this I notice that the leaves and vines are rich and healthy, but the roots are withered. Farther out on the fire escape there's a plant I've never seen before flowering with lush, white flowers.

real poem (happiness)

We're all fucked up because in English
the phrase "to make someone happy"
suggests that's possible.

good shoppers trampled a man
to death does laziness save lives?
I meant *my* laziness by which I mean
the many ways I keep my boys
alive & the few words I put aside
for later *Be kind* mothers say
to yourself and others this is
an old topic & the only one today
I want to trample my own heart
here they come: sudden onset
of the end of loneliness

real poem (no elegy)

You are okay. Still
okay. Stay that way.

public school dream

I'm running and running through a huge empty building at night in winter. This is the only way to exercise in inclement weather. I jump over students and backpacks, running laps around the gym. I don't feel anything—not the floor, or bleachers I bang into, not the effort of running. I'm not sweating. I'm dead.

[nature]

I stopped along a fence once
gathering wool from the starry
brambles a kind of *pitch*-

mark fence not like
the holocaust the dark
space where the earth is

wet maybe a shadow either
the place you've already
been or not been yet

at the edge of winter
the fox is thick *bushel*
fence *pockmark* fence *pain*

fence *knife* fence where-
ever there is nature at the end
is a fence no one looks at

the fox of what they see
but where the fox is white
he disappears   a girl's

pleated skirt her hand in
someone's she has braids
branches slice the sky

scrub brush only looks soft
usually a child forgets
the word I forgot was *barbed*

please alice notley tell me how to be old

but don't read this poem whose title implies I
think you're old but you are at least older than
me I don't just mean time passing though that
makes everyone old unless death & I don't
want *that* which is not to say I'm terrified but
don't not read this poem b/c you've died
I'd rather insult you what I mean is—oh look!
I think the rookie cops are graduating today
Times Square is a sea of blues there's a secret
staircase at the end of the shuttle platform that
takes me right to my therapist's office but you
don't live here anymore anyway Alice I haven't
got much time or maybe I have no one knows
I want to tell you that all the people who say
they love me are siphoning me feeding off me
not like they did when they were babies but
eating away at me & for a while my soul
seemed to fly out of my body but I didn't know
that's what had happened didn't know I was
a living dead they talk about in sci-fi books until
today when it flew back in & I woke up

w/ my soul intact the days & days of rain
made my city as clean as it can get I ran around
the bridle path not dressed warmly enough
like a good horse my breath soft & white I
listened to a podcast of dharma talks *May all
sentient beings feel and know happiness and
the causes of happiness* I do today feel happy
& now on the subway I just read your poem
"poem" that starts w/ your kids talking & thought
oh, children in poems! but you're old now &
maybe I am too we already lived that life w/ young
children while I was running I really felt happy felt
I knew the cause of happiness felt my soul had returned
to my body I shuddered to realize how like
a living dead I'd been you seem so alive to me
your language so human angry real happy & also
the cause of these things I'm passing the day care
now on a bus to pick up my middle son
my oldest boy's walking home alone which
he doesn't like to do how I must trust
the universe how it fills & siphons me but you
w/ your fuck-you beauty & siren song no
not *siren* you're not stopping the boats but rather
pushing us along what I want to know is how

to be old & strong & not care so much
by which I mean care *so* much as I do & always
will but not care about how much I care my
therapist asked *Do you lose a lot of hands in poker?*
& said I was a bad negotiator said I tolerate
too much emotional chaos & put the needs of others
before my own *What* I asked *is the alternative?*
he gave me nothing maybe b/c I'm a bad
negotiator? "how could a woman write an
epic?" you wrote "How could she now if she
were to decide the times called for one?" but *you
did* even though you wrote: women are more
likely to write something "lyrical (/elegiac) or
polemical, rather than epic or near-epic" so I'm
asking you not just how to be old but how
to be a woman as my girlhood if I ever had one
is over now really gone & the sharp fear I feel
when my son does not call when he said he would
—how can any mother write an epic when—my
fear receding behind his small-voiced apology (a
little nodule in my right breast) *safe*—when I'm
so terribly interruptible

baby dream

A birthday party is letting out. I look into a passing family's stroller. Before I say anything the parents ask, "Can we leave them with you?" Inside the stroller are five weird-looking babies, all jumbled up. Josh makes a noise that means he doesn't want these babies and finds them disgusting. "My husband—" I say, apologetically. "Fine," says the father. The parents take two of the babies, so I will only have to watch three. When I look up, the babies and the stroller are gone. I hear a car screech and see the stroller—actually just the chassis—lying overturned in the street. I run down the street and find the top part of the stroller. Filled with dread, I turn the stroller basket over. Inside are those three terrible babies, unharmed.

real poem (painting)

Woke up to find the primary markets
not so solid and my oldest son knows
almost everything necessary. A sound
like jujitsu startled me—was anything—?
It occurred to me all those poets were
high when they wrote—and I—oh dear,
dear transparency. All paintings are
an experiment of light in an empty
room. All paintings are is an experiment
of light in an empty room. I said that.

two kinds of suffering

if you want me to admit living in a city is
a disease I will admit it if someone said
I like being stoned all the time it's a perfectly good way
to live in fact it's the only way things seem real
to me would anyone approve? so that's one
analogy & when I go into the sobering world
of suburbs or country or if there still was
wilderness—let's pronounce it WILDER-NESS
and see if it might then exist—the disaster
of human progress I have just left is then
inescapably obvious *how could I? live like?* until
I crawl back into the peopled hive
& live the only real life I know

real poem (post-confessional)

Last night the Post-Confessional
Poet said, "I don't know how many
poets stand up at a reading and
tell you how bad they're doing—I'm
doing real bad." Later she said,
"Now we put toothbrushes up
assholes in poems all the time."

baby hospital dream

Women are milling about outside a hospital, waiting for their babies to be passed back to them through metal chutes in the brick wall. When I demand entry, the personnel in their starched whites ignore me. Other mothers milling about also ignore me. I wonder if they are hired actors. How can they be so calm? I sneak into the hospital and find my baby. He is a small mass of exposed muscle. He is a little chop, a brisket, on a metal pallet. My meat baby is surrounded by hundreds of meat babies all splayed out in hundreds of rooms off a quiet corridor.

pedestrian

don't want to go to the well-reviewed movie
The Maid at the Angelika or read Harryette
Mullen's *Recyclopedia* or eat chicken soup w/
roast chicken & egg noodles from Kelley & Ping
or buy anything in any superb boutique except
a slightly elliptical stoneware sugar bowl w/ a
smooth top & elegant spoon I've been
looking for that for years no one has that
or write a poem even though I vowed
to write one every day in November or walk
to the Asian grocery on Mott & Canal to buy
katsuobushi & rice sticks & usukuchi &
bamboo shoots & rice wine vinegar so I can
cook my way through the Momofuku cookbook
I've made pickled cauliflower so far which was delightful
I don't want to have coffee or not have coffee
or listen to the *This American Life* podcast on infidelity
which makes me tired b/c I don't want to have sex w/
anyone just want my dear husband to
read me *A Game of Thrones* by George RR Martin

while I lie in bed w/ a buckwheat eye pillow
are you scandalized by my admission of love
for genre fiction? where are our kids in this
fantasy? let's be movie parents whose kids never
intrude on the viewer's enjoyment I don't want
to stop at this espresso bar or that one or that one
or even live in NY anymore or go to the day care
before I teach at the 92nd St Y or not see my son
and feel guilty/trapped wonder why I don't live
in Maine or have more children or fewer or
how I feel about my parents or poetry or what
constitutes a 'practical decision' or finish reading
this *NY Times Mag* article about the Obamas'
marriage which I took w/ me in case I didn't
want to read Mullen I don't want these poetmom
e-mails w/ cute attachments of kids in Halloween
costumes I hate animals still shouldn't eat them
this hipster music makes me slightly suicidal
on the subway a discarded newspaper says
another NYU student got through the suicide
barrier at Bobst Library you know one can make
pickles w/ almost anything the radish
pinks everything up nicely but itself goes white

I don't like the expression 'in a pickle' to mean
fucked or *out of luck* or *stuck* or *down on luck*
as pickles are one of the few things I like
especially the daily transformation brought about
by sugar & salt & vinegar today I said *My tolerance*
for traveling through space & time is increasing daily
I think I was lying why do I imagine someone's
interviewing me sometimes they are & always
ask about my 'real life' & the 'juggling act' which is
stupid I'm not juggling my family like eggs or oranges
my bangs are too straight make me look androidal
I should stick to cutting my own hair is *this* writing
'work'? Donald Hall says so but I don't know
I've stayed on the local b/c why go nowhere faster
I'm paying for day care anyway so have 'free
time'—ha HA!— this is a kind of despair (not
needing to be/do anywhere/anything) (I could
disappear perhaps have) also an extravagance
for which we pay dearly—time—the toddler
puts in his time lives there really as I travel the city
hating poetry & my haircut & all the things I do not
want to do the man w/ maroon kerchief gives up
his seat for a large woman who now sits marking

sheet music what should I be doing? dying? I am I
have an idea for a website where mothers shoot
home movies & I upload them as part of my ongoing
project to 'accurately describe women's lives'
the woman next to me is reading an FSG book
can't see the title the man on her left snores
& leans into her please someone remind me what's
the point of literature? 72nd St & Cathy Wagner's
book *My New Job* includes the word PENIS frequently
that's nice & makes me feel happy like a pinked-up
pickled radish or maybe I should say 'pinked down'
since radishes start out red but lend their color
to the brine & neighboring veggies as they soak
Please! I'm not 'relating' this to the NYC subway
how vile of you to think so I told Matt
taking the shuttle at Times Square during rush hour
causes me serious distress a human tsunami perhaps
we deserve a large-scale population reduction
it seems inevitable I'm dehumanized by NY & my
proximity to others fatal loneliness of crowds
(reading or writing creates a private sphere
in a way that thinking can't) I sometimes wonder if
I actually have a self that's ridiculous you want to

witness stream of consciousness? Times Square's your
destination the Spanish lovely indecipherable noise
a pleasure not to understand I imagine it's not all
banal & meaningless like my own daily communication
of course those aren't synonyms the banal is often full
of meaning a woman coughs all over my air everyone's
scared to die except the people who aren't Jeremy said
Death as an idea is scary but as a process quite natural
I like him & the way he makes me feel smarter
than I am even though he doesn't like the way I respond
in interviews doesn't buy the James Schuyler line
I often quote "I have always been more interested
in truth than in imagination" Jeremy thinks I'm
selling myself short selling short is what Jeremy
as a hedge-fund manager actually does are these
associative games worth their weight in ink? he'd
sell this short I bet this poem's possibly timely
not likely timeless which someone once said
separates poetry from the pedestrian

[once you pass this point
you must continue to exit]

the plane opens its body to me I am alive
on the plane in the coffee shop in bed in traffic
among the living I'm leaking then cracking open

here here here the alive splinter in me our
neighborhood everywhere
   How are you? alive

How are you?   to be this this
tired one must be must be   what
do I even like to eat?   *How are you?*

She's I say   *The way she said*
my name my whole name when I called these details
make life unbearable & without which meaningless

i do not like your job

there's no chance you'll have sex w/ me
at 3:15pm which is 2 minutes from now
you're at the place called work & it takes
20–65 minutes to get home depending on
whether you drive or ride the subway anyway
you can't leave early b/c it's necessary to impress
the right people you'd like to stay at the place
called job & you're new so don't yet know who/m
to impress I suspect no one in the dept would
appreciate my desire to copulate at 3:15pm
& the 20–65-minute preparation that requires
truth is you didn't have a job for 10 years & we
never made love in the afternoon you don't like to
I do but it takes two I'm lying here reading poetry
which makes me horny I won't say whose (he *is*
a hunk) just the act of reading anything in the last
sweet silence of a toddler's nap this is
my WORK I suppose but utterly different from
yours I'm embarrassed to admit I just delighted myself
w/ 2 squares of dark chocolate this is one of the

10 DAYS OF AWE I like the way this poet writes about his wife I like a man hot for his wife I like a man w/ a guitar on stage that's someone's job but 'hot for his wife' isn't a profession not yours anyway that's why I hate your job

real poem (gay men don't snore)

is what I'd call a rock band or maybe
"Sarcastic Overdrive" or maybe . . .
Oh, look, even though you kept me up
all fucking night, we still love each other
enough to say, "Hey, that's a cool name
for a rock band."

brooklyn dream

Josh takes me to see a house in Brooklyn that he bought, on a whim, without consulting me. I don't know what to say. I don't like that the bed is right next to the front door. The doorbell chimes. I'm not dressed and have trouble finding something to wear. The place is filled with someone else's things. I hold a T-shirt against my chest and open the door for a man I've never seen before. More people arrive. I realize they are there for an open house and that we don't own this house after all. People tramp all over the house. I walk through the many rooms and out to the backyard. There is a huge lawn leading down to a massive lake. I hear a woman say to another woman, "We've got to put an offer on this right away!" I suddenly want this house very badly but know we can't afford it. I walk down to the water's edge. A tremendous serpent swims toward me along the surface of the water. Its head is as big as mine. Its body is thicker than my thigh. It moves so quickly—there's no way to outrun it. In seconds, the serpent reaches me and swallows my right arm up to my shoulder. I'm screaming but no one hears me over the sound of the water. I black out from the pain. When I come to I'm talking calmly with other people who are attending the open house. My arm looks fine, but I can feel that it's dead. I'll never be able to use it again.

wish you were here you are

time isn't the same for everyone there is
science behind this when you fly into space
you're not experiencing time at the same rate
as someone tethered to Earth & someone
moving quickly experiences time at a slower rate
even on Earth so as I run through Central Park
at a speed not much faster than walking but slightly
I am shattering fields of time around me
& experiencing time differently from those I pass
last night I saw my son's adult self &
in the same moment toddler self this really
happened he was playing "Wish You Were Here"
by Pink Floyd on his electric guitar & feeling it
he's 11 & in between 2 kinds of time on the verge
of worlds I think we are too you & I who are old
young women it's not all 'downhill from here' we are
here you are & I am & this beautiful moment our sons

real poem (appellation)

"Writing with My Shoes On" is
a title for a poem. "Then I Did
Something Stupid" is better
for a short story. The trash smells
because living things decompose
isn't the name of anything just
a way of describing these environs.
To say I miss you in French
one says *tu me manques* where
tu means "you." Do the French
miss less because their you is
there before them? Syntactical
high jinks: methinks Americans
don't miss the missed-one
so much as feel how absence
crowds the I. Today my others are
far from me. "I"—   is
the name of this feeling.

baby dream

Jeremy and Amy have a baby boy. When I visit I see that the baby is a newborn but sitting at a table in a little chair. The baby smiles and reaches for things. I feed the baby a small spoonful of broccoli and garlic. The baby looks surprised. It dawns on me that I've done something wrong. I wipe the broccoli off the baby's face and bring him to Amy. I make it seem as if the baby reached for the broccoli and put it in his mouth himself. "I can see it," she says as she opens the baby's mouth. There are several unchewed florets of broccoli as well as whole pieces of lettuce in the baby's mouth. We fish most of the food out of the baby's huge, Muppet-like mouth. I'm scared and embarrassed. "I don't know *anything* about the lettuce—" I say. The baby closes his mouth and becomes a Lego Transformer machine. I fiddle with the baby but can't find his mouth shape again. I want Amy to move the baby's soul to another machine but am afraid to ask her to try.

the body in health feels
so little pleasure
someone's

texting me
go away world
go away world disasters

I shake the frail vernacular
each week less
and fewer words

the self stripped
to the slender trembling I
escapes me

I hold babies
against a tsunami get
away Great Mother

who art so
insubstantial
you keep me

marred and lonesome
the sun pushes me
deeper into the earth

birds hysterical
in their nests trees
neither kind

nor menacing
sway in the tepid
wind I am

all bark no bud
or blossom
can break through

that great diaspora

I'll never leave New York & when I do
I too will be unbodied—what? you
imagine I might transmogrify? I'm from
nowhere which means here & so wade out
into the briny dream of elsewheres like
a released dybbuk but can't stand
the soullessness now everyone who ever
made sense to me has died & everyone I love
grows from my body like limbs on a rootless tree

real poem (personal statement)

I skim sadness like fat off the surface
of cooling soup. Don't care about
metaphor but wish it would arrive
me. There's a cool current of air
this hot day I want to ride.
I have no lover, not even my love.
I have no other, not even I.

paris dream

We're renting an apartment in Paris. Josh's mother is visiting but staying at a hotel. I'm eager to show her our place. I'm in bed and can hear the kids and Josh awake in the other room. I roll over and look out the large window. It's still early and quite dark—everything looks murky. I can see the lovely gray water and reeds. I'm surprised we were able to find a house like this in Paris. I can't imagine what body of water it is. It doesn't look like the Seine. It occurs to me to use Google Maps to see what this lake or river or pond or ocean is called, but I'm concerned about roaming charges. The water is right up against the window. A submerged car floats by. "Josh!" I scream but the word is a hoarse whisper. The kids and Josh are fighting. "We're sinking!" I shout over and over but no one hears me. The room tilts—the whole house suddenly at a strange angle. I can't get up. I'm concerned that if we try to swim out through a window, the released pressure will make the house sink faster. Josh might know what to do, but I can't reach him. We're going down fast.

[taking away taking away everything]

Once I said *I looked at paintings*
and had ideas could concentrate
Matisse was not an important painter

to me now less so everything less so
everything important this was
the last show I saw before

What I like I used to say *is process*
when there were still things
I liked   she is (I am not

exaggerating) bone fragments and ash
and still many countries away   *Unless*
you see with your own eyes they say

Get on a plane they say
You won't believe they say
How do you know someone asks

when a poem is finished? I have
nothing else to say it is not
easy no other subject every

day a version of today today is
day 29 I heard the flatline
over the phone   *This is*

the end I thought but it was already
over Dr Lin said   *Do I have your*
machine heart in the rain against

the Upper West Side where it is
always night for one day makes it
difficult to paint the rain

                              consent?
he said inside this terrible painting
the world goes on without any

open windows   in *The Dream*
Matisse takes away the plants
an urn or vase what looks

like wings in an effort to
condense the body into essential
lines you have taken everything

away   *I am still alive* says
the painting that was never alive
Matisse said the woman becomes

an angel in violet I do not believe
in this view I am a bowl
of apples in this view I am

Notre Dame in the rain am
an interior am the drapes
pulled open pulled *tight* I am

the tablecloth that looks like
my grandfather's tallis I am
the white of the cloth that looked like

my grandfather's tallis I am pressed
flat made shapely magnolia anemone
yellow-blue interior red with Egyptian

curtain fern interior interior
interior the incidental woman
now color shape no face at all

knock knock. who's there?
someone. someone who?

the bygone winds on top of everything new
president now scuds there their they're
out there did you hear about that poet's
daughter I can't even imagine instead again
watch a video he took of her at the beach
wind breaking apart her smart answer i.e.
fashion & feminism how could she? how how
how the wind is——is—is it this bad in
Brooklyn? can't breathe nights bad chest
my baby's past the average age of sids but
what's that whoop—no that's wind off the Hudson
rattling the high-rise I'm afraid to think too much
about his daughter as if she's contagious I want
something between her & my son & son & son
some promise they will not be harmed will not
launch scuds or be targeted or ever
by their own hand someone send me
some promise some proof

professor dream

I am a tenure-track professor in the English department. A group of three women call me over to their table. We're in a dining hall or a library. I'm pleased to be invited. These women are older and have never before given me the time of day. They begin to ask me questions about poetry and about my favorite poets. I try to impress them but they seem dissatisfied with my answers. "Do you mean to say the only job of a poet is to put words together in a way that makes them interesting?" asks one of the women. I start to answer—start to say something about how combinations of words are often interesting even without the poet doing very much—but it's strangely difficult to speak. I reach into my mouth and pull out a retainer that is connected to brackets and braces. I start pulling out the braces, hoping to be able to speak more easily. A thick strand of drool stretches from my mouth to my hand, which is full of small metal pieces. I say, "I'm muh moor arficulate when I'm theach'hing." "That's so passive!" one woman says, frowning at me. "Alice Notley is *very* aggressive and I *love* her!" I spit back. Men at a nearby table shush us loudly.

real poem (post-confessional 2)

No, wasn't me. She
was drunk or high and all
sexed up. Who picks her kids up
on time? I wondered.

just off the road near lynchburg, va

John says, *James Wright says* [something about
how a poet writing about the landscape is
always writing about himself]—I'm listening
but also standing on a bridge over railroad tracks
& watching some sort of woodchuck or muskrat
or groundhog scurry in & out of the hilly underbrush
so not listening closely *Yeah* I say *it's beautiful here
but I was writing city poems so* . . . how can I explain
to John I don't believe he exists don't believe
in Virginia or these horses or houses that tractor
lawnmower small mammal burrowing it is too
incredulous such simultaneous lives I'm not sure
the earth is round can't perceive that & the hills
of Virginia mean I can't see where I am except
right here *Old* mountains *Old* trees Laurel said
when I asked her why I love this landscape
even though I don't believe it exists even when
I'm standing in it *John* I say *I think James Wright
is full of shit* but I don't say that not even

as a joke not even over the phone I want to say
on this first day of spring our bodies will not
break into blossom I want to tell John I don't
believe in the bucolic or the pastoral I can't
believe it's possible to waste my life

hair dream

I reach up to touch my hair—there's something stuck, some sort of residue. When I run my fingers through my hair a large clump comes away in my hand. When I look in the mirror, the left side of my hair is thinner. Also, I'm wearing a sticker that says:

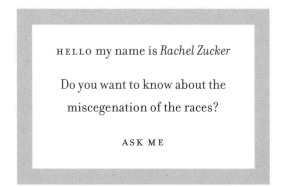

HELLO my name is *Rachel Zucker*

Do you want to know about the miscegenation of the races?

ASK ME

real poem (workshop)

In class Eddie used the word *cunt*
twice in a poem. The girls said, "We
do not like this cunt. We *do* like *this*
cunt—the cunt in 'cunteenth time.'"
But "*dirty* cunt" they did not like.
Boystar said, "It's *supposed* to be nasty."
But the girls said, "If you want a female
audience not to hate you—" I said,
"Has anyone heard of Lenny Bruce?"
The girls said, "Well, there are ways
of being offensive and there are *ways*
of being offensive." Boystar and Eddie
wore half-smiles like Mona Lisa.
We crowded around Eddie's poem
and picked it apart. I said, "You made
everyone break the rules—*that's*
something." Afterward Eddie said,
"I don't *usually* write like that." I didn't
know whether he meant using *cunt* in a poem

twice or something else because it was
the first poem of his I'd ever read.
Either way, what's really *déclassé*
is writing about students.

i'm nobody you are too

oh Metropolitan today I'm sick of your slapstick
paintings of naked babes by which I mean women
even Georgia O'Keeffe how much Alfred loved her
rankles me I'm a lesser husband's wife & succumb
to jealousy even the modern stuff's no-go in this bad
mood yesterday the interactive IBM THINK show
told me we have MORE WAYS OF SEEING THAN
EVER BEFORE & more technology to MEASURE
BELIEVE & ACT I don't believe that crap INTERACTIVE
means press a panel it tells you what to think I think
we've got too many people & no genetically modified
grain of rice can fix that I do like how Lucian Freud
puts paint on canvas *look!* that man's hand looks like
an extra cock! how nice! a woman walks by
in an EAT SLEEP READ t-shirt last week DA Powell
via Skype told my undergrads he had no blueprint
for a poem *It's language going through my body*
and the poem is what I hang on to he said Whitman's line
helped him *Reach into the gutter and create a horizon*
for the eye he said *The end is also a doorway for what*

comes after I almost just fell down b/c Kiki Smith's *Lilith*
a feral beast-woman crouched on the wall b/t Modern
& Contemporary her breasts & flash of green eyes
almost tripped me *The flaws* said DA *allow us to see*
the poem's beauty he said *I'm not so interested in poets*
as I am in poetry oh dear I think I'm more interested in
thinking about people making things than in looking at
the things they make *Poetry speaks to the irrational part*
of ourselves that's DA again but I'm sick of poetry &
my students the museum & art & everything what I'm
looking forward to if you must know is jury duty where
no one can bother me my civic responsibility a modern
mother's rubber room no ekphrasis allowed nothing
to do nothing to look for look at *Write about that* I snap
at no one DA might like what I write in my notebook:
SHE ALMOST FELL ON HER POSTERIORITY THANKS
TO KIKI SMITH by SHE I mean me I'm a big shot
in this crap museum I'm no one too

public school dream

I go to pick Moses up from school. While I'm waiting for him,
a teacher walks by and tells me Moses is going to get the highest
GPA in his grade. I'm pleased. I notice, though, that all the kids
were dismissed and have gone home, and I get nervous. I go up
to the receptionist and ask where he is. She asks me his name—
all of a sudden, I can't remember. I'm mortified. The recep-
tionist mocks me by mimicking my facial gestures. "Isn't it
YOUR responsibility to make sure the kids get home safely?" I
say. "Not if a parent don't even know her own kid's name!" she
says. A teacher tries to help—"Is his name Moses?" she asks.
"We were going to name him that," I say, "but we didn't." I re-
member, then, that his name is Adam Birenbaum.

the meanest thing i ever said

my middle son's friend's little sister died
& I cried & began to cough I had a bad
virus when this happened could barely
speak for days to say this bad bad news
the girl the same age as my littlest son felt
right somehow to have my throat on fire
chest crushing my breath & wallow in this
sorrow watching John Keats cough himself
to death in the movie *Bright Star* & lie
in a half-dark room reading a book called
Us about two old people moving toward
death I cried & wondered why my 95-year-old
demented grandmother didn't die instead
she hasn't said a word to anyone for years
& even when she still made sense had mental
faculties never had a nice word for anyone
April turned to May & I went out still wan
& weak to sit on a bench in the sun & saw
the cherry trees & magnolias & nonfruiting
Bradford pear trees lavishing & letting down

their petals all over the unworthy city
& into the open faces of tulips that had been
planted for our pleasure only & cried
through my hot throat at this bio-opulence
this floral understory b/c the little girl's
real name was Blossom & she really died
cruel, cruel I thought until slowly my strength
came back & my voice day by day so today
when I saw Matt & Wayne & they asked
How are you? I said *Terrific actually*

resort dream

I'm at a hotel in a Third World country. War breaks out. Many of the tourists get out, go home, but days later I'm still there. Across the bay I watch as an event occurs. Smoke covers the night sky. I've got to get out. My father is with me. We start running. As we run, the people around us change. They're Japanese! They're Haitian! They're Hawaiian! We run. We get to a plane. On the plane the only person I know is my stepsister's husband. I'm dispassionate about his survival, almost indifferent. The plane is attacked. We shoot through the air like a missile. People are thrown about the cabin for what seems like hours. I am strangely calm. Either my children are safely elsewhere or never existed or are already killed. I'm neither afraid nor grief-stricken. When we hit the water I think, "More people died," and I say to my stepbrother-in-law, "It's time to *get out*." The water is spraying into the plane through tiny cracks in the walls. I stop a uniformed crewman and ask the way out. At first he lies to me but by watching his eyes I figure out the real directions. The crew is misdirecting passengers because there isn't time for everyone to escape. On my way to the exit I pass a man pushing a baby in a stroller.

The man is weeping. "Your wife died?" I ask him. He nods. I point toward the real exit. He is skeptical. I say, "You couldn't be of less use to me," which makes him trust me. When we reach the exit I see that the baby is disfigured. I don't care. I don't care about anything or anyone. That's why we will survive. I have never been so powerful.

an airplane stitches
the gray sky   *there*
not-there *there* the city's
coyness trembles
through me   Carl Jung
lost his mind looking for
his soul   I'd run at you
with readied spear but
the spears are rungs
in a metal fence spiked
against settling birds
my mind is made up
of you   what would you
have of me?

My appreciation to the editors of the following, who published (often in different forms) excerpts from this book: *American Poetry Review*, *Body*, *Bone Bouquet*, *Court Green*, *Epiphany*, *Everyday Genius*, *Front Porch*, *H_ngm_n*, *Kenyon Review*, *The Literary Review*, *Low Ball*, *Phantom Limb*, *Ploughshares*, *Plume*, *Poets.org*, *Poor Claudia*, *Spoon River Review*, *Virginia Quarterly*, *Washington Square*, and *Women's Electronic Poetry Anthology*.

Abounding gratitude to the following readers who offered advice and support for one or both manuscripts: Joshua Goren, Sheila Heti, Deborah Landau, Erika Meitner, Geoffrey Nutter, DA Powell, Matt Rohrer, Craig Morgan Teicher, Daniel Shiffman, Laurel Snyder, Darin Strauss, and Matthew Zapruder. Thank you also to the National Endowment for the Arts for support during the time of writing and editing this book.

Thank you to my friends and family, especially my husband, Joshua Goren, and my children: Moses, Abram, and Judah.